New  Heart, New Mind

Renewing Our Minds

by the Power of the Spirit

the WORD
among us

The Word Among Us Press

9639 Doctor Perry Road

Ijamsville, Maryland 21754

ISBN: 0-932085-65-2

Cover design by Christopher Ranck

Made and printed in the United States of America.

Contents

Introduction

I n the early church, once believers were baptized in the name of Jesus and received the Holy Spirit, they faced a whole new set of challenges: Their minds needed to be renewed by the power of the Holy Spirit. For years, these new Christians had been formed by the values and philosophies of the world around them, both good and bad. Now that they had met Christ, however, everything began to change. They had received new hearts in baptism, but in many ways they still had to deal with their old minds. This is why St. Paul told the Ephesians, "Put off your old nature which belongs to your former manner of life and is corrupt through deceitful lusts, and be renewed in the spirit of your minds, and put on the new nature, created after the likeness of God" (Ephesians 4:22-24).

If we think about the way parents try to raise their children, we can get a sense of why God takes the renewal of our minds so seriously. Every mother or father loves to see their children fulfill all the promise within them, in terms of health, academics, friendships, sports, faith, and a whole host of other areas. Likewise, parents suffer when their children are hindered in their growth and development. How much more does God our Father love to see us grow into the children he created us to be! He wants all of us to learn how to walk in true holiness, love, and faith. He even suffers whenever our potential is stifled.

The mere thought of such a thorough renewal of our thoughts and desires can sound awfully intimidating. But the good news is that it's not up to us alone! While it does require our genuine desire and cooperation, this renewal only takes place through the comfort, guidance, and power of the Holy Spirit who lives in us. We don't renew ourselves—God renews us as we surrender to him!

In this little book, we will explore this process of renewal and growth in holiness. No matter how holy or sinful we may feel, each of us is on the same path of discipleship. So if, as you read, you see habits or mindsets in yourself that need to change, praise God! It means that he is already at work in you, changing you a little bit more into the disciple of Christ he created you to be. As you cooperate with the Spirit, be sure to cry out to Jesus for strength and wisdom. Listen closely as he whispers words of guidance and wisdom to your heart. Above all, never forget his promise: "I am with you always, to the end of the age" (Matthew 28:20).

Jeff Smith
The Word Among Us

Clean Out the Rust!

**As the Holy Spirit moves in us,
we will develop a new perspective.**

*Do not be conformed to this world but be
transformed by the renewal of your mind, that
you may test and prove what is the will of God,
what is good and acceptable and perfect.
(Romans 12:2)*

Have you ever noticed how much damage
rust can do to a car? In many cases, if it's
left too long, it can eat away at the metal
so much that a simple repainting isn't enough for a
proper repair. Instead, the whole rusted area needs to

be cut out and replaced with new metal.

In our lives, we all have a certain amount of "rust" as well—not the rust of deteriorating metal, but the rust of mindsets that are opposed to God. Just as rust in a car is the result of water going where it doesn't belong and remaining there too long, so the rust in our lives is the result of sinful thoughts and actions finding a place in us and being allowed to stay too long.

More often than not, sins we commit or problems we face are symptoms of something deeper going on in our minds. For instance, when we lash out at someone in anger, our actions are prompted by the way we have learned to respond when things don't go our way or when our expectations are not being met. Or, when we have bitterness against a loved one, it often comes from the way we have interpreted a situation—correctly or incorrectly. In short, when the normal events of life in this world set off negative or sinful behavior in us, it should be a sign to us that there's some "rust" in us that needs to be dealt with.

God Wants to Renew Our Lives. The promise of the gospel is that God wants to transform the way we think and act. He wants to remove all the rust and make us good as new, and this happens as we learn to live "in the Spirit" (Romans 8:9; 1 Peter 4:6). Living in the Spirit simply means allowing God to strengthen and raise up our good habits and to change and transform our bad habits. It means being open to the Holy Spirit's words of affirmation of the good within us and asking him to prick our consciences concerning the areas that need change.

St. Paul told the Christians in Rome, "Do not be conformed to this world but be transformed by the renewal of your mind, that you may test and prove what is the will of God, what is good and acceptable and perfect" (Romans 12:2). The renewal that Paul wrote about is something different from conversion. Conversion is our initial decision to give our lives to Jesus, and it's closely related to what happened to us when we were baptized. Renewal, on the other hand, has more to do with the ongoing changes God wants to make in our lives after our initial conversion—the call to holiness that he has given each one of us.

The parable of the prodigal son (Luke 15:11-32) is mostly a story about conversion. Finally coming to his senses, the prodigal son decides that he will return to his father and ask his forgiveness (15:18). The love and riches that the father lavishes on his son is a beautiful image of the way God receives any one of us who turns to him in repentance and conversion.

But the story doesn't end there, and the rest of the parable focuses on the renewal that God wants to do in the lives of all Christians (Luke 15:25-32). When he sees how his father treats this prodigal son, the boy's older brother gives way to jealousy, anger, and resentment. This son lived in his father's house. He was obedient to his father's commands and never sinned as dramatically as his brother had. Still, he had a number of "rusty" mindsets that needed to be cut out and renewed.

That's the way it is with us as well. We have been baptized. We believe that Jesus has saved us. We have the promise of eternal life. Yet, like the older son, we all have a number of patterns of thought and action that need to be changed or renewed.

Transformed into His Likeness. In another para-ble, Jesus told his listeners to put the "new wine" of the Holy Spirit into new "wineskins" (Matthew 9:17). Why? Because the old wineskins are weak and inflexible. If new wine is poured into them, they will only burst, and the new wine will be lost. In other words, our old ways of thinking and acting have some weaknesses to them and need to be replaced with new ways.

Paul once said that as we gaze at the glory of the Lord—in prayer, at Mass, or on the faces of our loved ones and the needy—we are being changed into his likeness (2 Corinthians 3:18). But he also said that our gazing on the Lord, and so our ability to be transformed into his likeness, is hindered by "veils" that lie over our minds (3:15).

This is our challenge. We can be transformed by the power of the Holy Spirit. We can come to see more and more of the glory, the power, and the love of God. But this only happens as the veils are removed, as the "rust" is cut away. Our challenge is to keep all of our strong points and to allow God to transform all of our weak points. It's to remove every hindrance so that we can see Jesus more clearly and so be changed more fully.

Our Relationship with Jesus. Our God wants to have a warm and loving relationship with each of us. He wants to teach us to live in the Spirit because he knows that when we stay close to the Holy Spirit we will be transformed into his image more and more.

Growing in our relationship with Jesus is a two-step process. On God's side, the Holy Spirit is working each day to teach and transform us. On our side, we have the ability to say "yes" or "no" to the Spirit. When we say "no," we are telling God that we can handle our lives better on our own. When we say "yes" and yield to the Holy Spirit, we are telling God that we need and want his help. This is the best way to be transformed and renewed. This is the best way to build our relationship with Jesus. This is the best way we will fall ever deeper in love with him.

Transformed into Christ

Three Practical Steps

1. BE FILLED BY GOD. There is a big difference between an empty gas tank and a full one. Likewise, God wants us to be regularly filling up on his grace, not running on empty. There are many ways to fill ourselves up with God, including reading and meditating on Scripture, praying and singing to God, and asking the Holy Spirit to reveal the wisdom of God to us. Probably the best way to be filled up with Jesus is to receive the Eucharist with an open heart.

2. LISTEN FOR THE HOLY SPIRIT. It's the Spirit's job to take our virtues such as kindness, love, and generosity and prune off any "dead branches" so that we will bear more fruit. He wants to make us more loving, more thoughtful, more generous, and more like Jesus—and he does this by giving us divine grace. All he asks is that we listen for his promptings and learn to rely on his power.

As the Holy Spirit moves in us and opens up new desires in our hearts, we will begin to develop a new perspective. For instance, we might find ourselves wanting to relate to our spouse and our children in a new way. We might develop a new desire to reach out to the poor or the sick. We might begin to suffer more over the murders, the abortions, and the injustices in the world. More than anything else, we might find our hearts reaching out to Jesus and loving him in a new and more profound way.

3. PRACTICE REPENTANCE. Sin is like a clogged drain. When a drain is clogged, water cannot flow freely. Sin is also like the static that we hear when our radio reception is poor. The static prevents us from hearing the music or the news clearly.

If you want to unclog the drain, you can. If you want to get rid of the static, you can. If you want to be transformed and have your mind renewed, you can—through repentance. Repentance "unclogs the drain" so that the grace and love of God can flow freely into your heart. Repentance "clears up the static" so that you can hear God's voice and speak to him more freely.

Before you go to bed each night, turn your heart to Jesus and ask him to forgive you your sins. At Mass, take a moment during the Penitential Rite to reflect on your sins and ask Jesus to forgive you and shower you with his grace. When you go to confession, ask Jesus to wipe away every sin.

God wants us to turn to him so that our sins might be wiped away and so that we might experience times of refreshment from the Lord (Acts 3:19-20). God loves us so much that he will always forgive us. He welcomes every one of us home with open arms, just as the father welcomed the prodigal son. He is always ready to give us his love and his refreshment.

Developing Your Spiritual Instincts

**God wants to influence
the way we think and act.**

*My sheep hear my voice, and I know them, and
they follow me; and I give them eternal life, and
they shall never perish, and no one shall snatch
them out of my hand. (John 10:27-28)*

C asey is a collie who loves his family very much. Judging from his actions, you'd think he wants nothing more than to be with them all the time. He sits with them when they watch television, jumps up every time someone heads for the front door, and is a constant presence at every family meal. To the degree that a dog is capable of love, Casey loves his family.

Now, Casey's brain is only about as big as a tennis ball, so he's capable of only a few different thoughts at a time. And yet, whatever situation he's in, his one controlling thought seems to focus on being a member of the family. It's as if it were his natural instinct.

Spiritual Instincts. Jesus tells us that he is the Good Shepherd and that his sheep hear his voice and follow him (John 10:27). When a sheep perceives that his shepherd loves him and will guide and protect him, his instincts tell him to trust that shepherd and listen to his voice. In a similar way, we humans also have instincts—both natural and spiritual—that enable us to recognize *Jesus* and hear *his* voice.

When we look at the beauty of nature, it seems we naturally conclude that there must be a God (Romans 1:20). The vast expanse of the night sky tells us how immense and all-encompassing God must be. The power of the ocean waves tell us how strong God must be. In so many ways, our natural instincts point us to the truths about God. But while our natural instincts tell us that there must be a God, our spiritual instincts—when they are energized by the Holy Spirit—encourage us to *seek intimacy* with God. These instincts tell us that there is no greater joy than to sense the presence of God in our lives, to know his wisdom, and to experience his love.

In one sense, our spiritual instincts are similar to Casey's instincts for his family. Because of our spiritual instincts, we all have a desire to grow closer to God and to seek his love and affection. They tell us that it's worthwhile to spend time with God and they move us to obey his commands.

You would think that, with such positive instincts, we would have no problem getting to know God better. But our spiritual instincts face some serious obstacles. First, it's all too easy for our natural instincts to dominate our spiritual instincts and drown out the voice of the Spirit within us. Second, it's not uncommon for everyday life to convince us that we can get by with just a small amount of hope or peace. Finally, the devil is always at work, trying to convince us that we really don't need God's love or guidance.

If you put all this together, it's not hard to see how our instincts for God can become dulled. Since Casey is almost completely earthbound, we can't expect him to rely on anything but his natural instincts. But when we remain earthbound, our spiritual instincts grow dull and we miss out on a vital component of the life God intended for us. As we lose touch with God's plan for our lives and go without the comfort of his presence, our deepest interior needs—especially our needs for divine love and the peace that it produces—are left unfulfilled.

Spirit and Soul. Let's take a moment to stand back from the demands of daily life and take a look at the way God created our minds. We all have certain faculties: an intellect, a host of emotions, the ability to make decisions, a conscience, an imagination, an intuition, and a memory. Because we are created in the image of God, each of these faculties has both a natural dimension and a spiritual dimension. These two dimensions are meant to work very closely together, to the point where it is often difficult, if not impossible, to determine whether a good thought or a good act comes from the natural dimension of our minds or from the spiritual dimension.

A few examples from the life of St. Peter bear this out. On one occasion, Peter told Jesus, "You are the Christ," and Jesus replied, "Flesh and blood has not revealed this to you, but my Father who is in heaven." A few moments later, however, Peter tried to convince Jesus to avoid the cross, and Jesus said, "Get behind me, Satan!" (Matthew 16:15-17,21-

23). On another occasion, Peter told Jesus, "Even if I must die with you, I will not deny you," and yet on that same night, he pretended he didn't even know Jesus (26:35,69-74).

In all four instances, it was clearly Peter who was speaking and acting. Yet, in each instance, he was influenced by different forces: the Father in heaven, Satan, his own human sense of nobility, and his emotional sense of fear. So many different influences were vying for Peter's attention that we might wonder how he grew in holiness at all. But if we trace Peter's life, we can see that his spiritual instincts grew and matured over time. His natural instincts increasingly came under the influence of his spiritual instincts, to the point where he freely gave up everything for Jesus.

This is God's promise to us as well. He wants to transform and renew every one of us. He wants to influence the way we think and act so that we become just like him. He wants to teach us to look to him for wisdom, guidance, and love. We can be sure that if we seek him, we will certainly find him. After all, if he can do it for Peter, John, and all the saints, he can do it for us as well.

It is true that we now see only a "dim reflection" of who God truly is, but that in heaven we will see him face to face. It's also true that now we can know only a part of the mystery of God and his love, "but that in heaven we will know it fully" (1 Corinthians 13:12). But even within the limitations of our lives here on earth, we can be continuously transformed *here and now*. Jesus has already died for our sins. He has already sent his Holy Spirit. We don't have to wait. Perhaps we will see a limited reflection of God, but as we submit to the Spirit, that reflection can become clearer day by day.

The Process of Renewal. We know that everything we experience in this world comes into our minds through our senses of touch, smell, hearing, taste, and sight. Let's call these our "outer senses." As we go about our daily lives, these outer senses send information to our minds. The "input" is then met by our faculties (intellect, emotion, will, conscience, imagination, intuition, and memory) for storage and interpretation.

We know that our minds have been filled with a number of patterns and attitudes—some of them good, and some not so good. So, when we experience an event in our outer senses, it is interpreted by our minds based on its own merit, but also according to our personal memories and patterns of thought—good and not so good. Once the mind interprets the event, an action follows, whether it is a gesture we make, words we speak, or a decision to act in a certain way.

This is where the spiritual dimension comes into play. In every situation we face, the Holy Spirit wants to confirm and raise up all of our good memories and patterns and he wants to heal and transform all of our bad memories and patterns. God looks at every situation as another opportunity for his Spirit to take us one step closer to him. He is always looking for opportunities to take the right ways we think and act and make them better as well as eliminate or change the wrong ways we think and act.

Transformed by the Power of God. Often it is difficult to say with confidence whether a specific thought or action came from the spiritual dimension or the natural dimension. They work so closely together that there is often no way of separating them. But whatever the source, the fruit we bear is a clear sign of whether we are being influenced and renewed by the Holy Spirit. Either we will find ourselves thinking and acting in the "same old way," or in a whole new way.

When all is said and done, if we are thinking and acting according to the "same old way," then we have to admit that we are not allowing the Holy Spirit to transform us and renew us. If, however, we are displaying ever increasing degrees of love, compassion, generosity, and peace, we can be confident that we are being changed into the likeness of God. Further, when we see negative patterns such as anger, resentment, envy, or selfishness diminish, we can take heart that God is transforming us into his likeness.

God wants to renew each of us with his love. He wants to satisfy our spiritual instincts. He wants to make us new in the attitudes of our minds so that we can become more like Jesus (Ephesians 4:23-24). With God's help, everything is possible—even the complex task of renewing our minds.

The Way of Daily Transformation

Advice from Spiritual Masters

Holiness is not a matter of any one particular method of spirituality. It is a disposition of the heart that makes us small and humble within the arms of God, aware of our weakness, but almost rashly confident in his Fatherly goodness.

— *Thérèse of Lisieux*

The human heart is torn between a sense of emptiness and a need of being filled, like the water pots of Cana. The emptiness comes from the fact that we are human. The power of filling belongs only to him who ordered the water pots filled. . . . Hence all perfect love must end on the note: "Not my will, but yours be done, O Lord."

— *Archbishop Fulton J. Sheen*

Grant me always to desire and to choose whatever is most acceptable to you, O Lord. Let my will always follow your will and agree perfectly with it. Let me not be able to will or not to will anything other than what you will or do not will."

— *Thomas à Kempis*

Be Transformed

The Holy Spirit works together with our spirit
—Romans 8:16

So that we can be transformed by the renewal of our minds
— Romans 12:2

Then we can test and approve what is God's will
—Romans 12:2

Then we can put off our old ways of thinking
—Ephesians 4:22

And be made new in the attitudes of our minds
—Ephesians 4:23

And put on a new self, resembling God in righteousness and holiness
—Ephesians 4:24

New Heart, New Mind

We can be set free from long-standing patterns of sin.

While he was yet at a distance, his father saw him and had compassion, and ran and embraced him and kissed him. (Luke 15:20)

It had been a very emotional day for the young man. He had just come back home after months of living on his own. He thought it would be so much fun to take his inheritance and explore the world, but it didn't take long before he got caught up in the wrong crowd and spent nearly every penny he had. After filling his days with riotous parties, fast women, and heavy drinking, he was humiliated, exhausted, and broken. The time had come to return home.

He wasn't expecting much. He was only hoping that his father would allow him to work as a hired hand on his farm. Even the thought of showing his face back there again was hard to swallow, but he had no other choice. He was convinced of one thing: It wouldn't be pleasant.

How wrong he was! His father was so happy to see him he wouldn't even let him finish his over-rehearsed speech. Throwing his arms around him, he showered his son with hugs and kisses and called for a huge party. A robe for his emaciated body, a ring for his grubby finger, even sandals for his bruised and weary feet—his father simply couldn't stop lavishing expensive gifts on him. Even his older brother's protests couldn't spoil the day. He had been welcomed back home, and it felt good.

But the next day was different, as were many of the days after that. The young man had changed so much during his time away that he didn't know how he would adapt to life at home. He'd spent so many months indulging every passion and following every false promise of happiness that he wasn't sure he would be able to survive in the peaceful, hard-working environment his father had created. Clearly, he would have to change a lot of his habits and attitudes, and that wouldn't be easy. But he also knew it was well worth it.

A Full Transformation. We're all familiar with the parable of the prodigal son and its lessons about conversion and the mercy of God (Luke 15:11-32). But if we use our imaginations and try to picture the challenge that the young man faced "the day after," we can get a glimpse into the challenges that all of us face every day.

Just as the prodigal son had to learn a new way of living and take on a new set of attitudes, so too does God want to renew our minds and teach us a new way of living. Both this beautiful parable and our own experience tell us that an initial change of heart isn't going to give us all the strength we need to face the challenges and demands of life in this world. Even more importantly, such an experience is just the beginning of a lifetime of God showing us more and more of his love for us.

How easy it can be, after having a deep experience of God's love at Mass, during confession, or in the quiet of our personal prayer, to feel as if everything is fine—at last! We feel surrounded by God's love, burdens are lifted, and guilt is washed away. Like the prodigal son on the day of his return home, life seems to be going our way. But then, we are surprised when temptation returns, perhaps even stronger than before; or when we realize that we are still struggling with the same sins as before. And we wonder why.

A New Heart and a New Mind. As one spiritual writer from the late nineteenth century put it, we may have experienced a new heart, but we still have our old minds—and that's what needs to be changed. We may begin our Christian lives with a narrow mind that can't tolerate people with differing viewpoints. Or, we may have little concern for the cries of the poor and needy.

Or, we may be like the prodigal son, unable to refuse the temptations of our fallen nature and the allure of the world. But God knows that if these attitudes are left alone, they will lead to deeper and deeper sin and draw us further and further away from his love. He knows—and he wants us to understand—that "the mind that is set on the flesh is hostile to God" (Romans 8:7).

The promise of the gospel is that we can be increasingly set free from the attitudes, philosophies, and limitations of a mind locked in sin. God wants to change us over time so that we become more and more like Jesus. He wants to make us all into a reflection of the love and power of Christ in this world. Let's take a look at how it happens.

Reflecting on the change that occurs in us when we are baptized, St. Paul told the Romans, "Consider yourselves dead to sin and alive to God in Christ Jesus" (Romans 6:11). To the Galatians, he wrote, "I have been crucified with Christ; it is no longer I who live, but Christ who lives in me" (Galatians 2:20). Such promising words! Such hopeful statements of freedom! But Paul also warned the Galatians, "Do not use your freedom as an opportunity for self-indulgence" (Galatians 5:13). He told the Romans, "Do not let sin reign in your mortal bodies" (Romans 6:12).

Put Off the Old Nature. Paul understood that if we want to experience true freedom in Christ, our minds need to be renewed, not just our hearts, and this happens as we draw near to the cross. That's why he told the Christians in Ephesus, "Put off your old nature which belongs to your former manner of life and is corrupt through deceitful lusts, and be renewed in the spirit of your minds" (Ephesians 4:22-23). He wanted them to understand that the salvation they received included not only a new heart—a heart filled with love from God—but also the renewal of *every aspect of their minds*.

The same is true for us today. God doesn't want us to accept our salvation in a general and vague way. The salvation that we received in baptism and the new life that we may taste at moments of blessing and conversion needs to be "worked out" to the point where it influences all our thoughts, motivations, and decisions. God wants to transform us to such a degree that all of our talents and abilities, all of our words and actions, become pure reflections of his life, his love, and his power.

Do you believe that your old life was crucified on the cross with Jesus? Do you believe that he wants to free you from every aspect of sin and darkness? When he died, Jesus passed judgment on our fallen lives. Now, he calls us to exercise our wills daily and "put off" every aspect of this old life—including our old ways of thinking.

A Divine Exchange. Every day, God invites us to the foot of the cross, where we can lay aside our old, fallen mentalities and trust him to give us a new mind. Day by day, he seeks to renew our minds so that we can become a whole new creation in him. Day by day, he wants his life to replace our old lives so that we can be sources of his light and refreshment to our families, our neighbors, our friends, and even our enemies. But the putting off—the denial, the forsaking, the crucifying—of our old mind is something that he calls us to do. This is why he has given us his Holy Spirit—not just to pour the love of God into our hearts, but also to strengthen our wills and purify our minds.

We can be confident that if we call out to the Spirit for the strength to do our part, God will do his part and bring us into greater and greater freedom. In many cases, we won't even know how he will do it; we may not even "feel" different right away. But if we look back over time, we will clearly see a difference. We will have a greater peace. We will be able to love people whom we couldn't love before. We will be more patient, kind, and generous toward those around us. The pain of past hurts will begin to melt away, only to be replaced by forgiveness and trust in God.

Our heavenly Father loves us too much to ever abandon us. Every time we say "no" to sin, he pours out divine grace. Every time we ask his forgiveness or turn away from temptation, he is up in heaven, cheering with all the angels and saints (Luke 15:7). Every time we reach out to a brother or sister in need, he throws his arms around the ones we are caring for—and he embraces us as well—just as the father embraced his long-lost son.

In Summary

Clean out the rust . . .

Living in the Spirit simply means allowing God to strengthen and raise up our good habits and to change and transform our bad habits.

Develop your spiritual instincts . . .

When we remain earthbound, our spiritual instincts grow dull and we miss out on a vital component of the life God intended for us.

A new heart, a new mind . . .

The promise of the gospel is that we can be increasingly set free from the attitudes, philosophies, and limitations of a mind locked in sin.